This Inspiring

C000193059

If found plec

My top three priorities are:

	WORK	LIFE
1		
2		
3		

I am grateful for the following in my work and life:

TOP TIPS FOR INSPIRING WOMEN LEADERS

The Pocket Book of Wisdom

Leigh Bowman-Perks &
Jonathan Bowman-Perks MBE

Fisher King Publishing

TOP TIPS FOR INSPIRING WOMEN LEADERS

Copyright © 2017 Leigh & Jonathan Bowman-Perks

Fisher King Publishing Ltd,
The Studio,
Arthington Lane,
Pool in Wharfedale,
LS21 1JZ,
England.

Cartoons by Roger Penwill

A CIP catalogue record of this book is available
from the British Library
ISBN 978-1-910406-60-1

www.fisherkingpublishing.co.uk

You will see our branding contains flying geese, which epitomises what we believe about inspirational leadership.

Here are a few of the reasons why:
As each goose flaps its wings it creates an 'uplift' for the birds that follow. By flying in a 'V' formation, the whole flock adds 71% greater flying range than if each bird flew alone.

When a goose falls out of formation, it suddenly feels the drag and resistance of flying alone. It quickly moves back into formation to take advantage of the lifting power of the bird immediately in front of it.

When the lead goose tires, it rotates back into the formation and another goose flies to the point position.

The geese flying in formation honk to encourage those up front to keep up their speed.

When a goose gets sick or wounded, two geese drop out of formation and follow it down to help and protect it. They stay with it until it dies or is able to fly again. Then, they launch out with another formation or catch up with the flock.

Like the geese, we must now leverage our full power and influence to create the 'uplift' so that others can follow and more inspiring women can succeed in leadership!

Alison Nimmo
CEO, The Crown Estate

Jasmine Whitbread
CEO, London First

Rt Hon Dame Tessa Jowell MP DBE
House of Commons, Westminster

Sara Thornton, CBE, QPM
British Police Officer & Chair of NPCC

Wendy Kunc
Jennifer Osbaldestin
MD, BAE Systems

Deputy Assistant Secretary
US Navy

Besty Hawkings
Director, Governance Initiative
The Democracy Fund

Ahood Al-Zaabi
Director of Government Affairs,
U.A.E. Embassy, U.S.

Hannah Parr
Lecturer

Fiona Lambert
Director, Dunelm

The Right Revd Rachel Treweek
Bishop of Gloucester

Annette Barnes
MD , Lloyds

Kate Cheetham
Group General Counsel &
Co-Chair Breakthrough

Dame Anne Pringle,
British Diplomat

Mercy Tembon
Director, World Bank

Lucy Brooker
Leadership Coach, RBS

Lady Susan Rice CBE,
President Scottish Council for Development & Industry

Amanda Jones
Sales & Marketing Director
Elliott UK

Jaz Rabadia MBE
Snr Manager, Starbucks Coffee Company

Julie Winkley
Assistant Director of Finance,
NHS

Dr. Claire Vink
Researcher and Consultant

Nathan Newton-Willington
Personal Trainer & Nutrition Coach

Jessamy McGregor
Diversity & Inclusion Manager,
MUFG

Emilie West
Wellbeing, Image & Brand
Consultant

Alanadh Wickham
Project Manager, ILT

With special thanks to the inspiring women leaders who have
contributed tips, techniques and words of wisdom for the book.

Contents

This book is a special edition and extended version of Top Tips for Inspiring Leaders, created in celebration of International Women's Day and inspirational women making a positive impact in their lives, organisations and communities.

About this book

We always encourage our leaders to keep things simple. Consequently, in this book, we are practicing what we preach! We want to help you become an even more successful and inspiring leader, yet with less effort.

By sharing some of the wisdom that we have collected from our research, and whilst coaching and developing inspiring women leaders, you can tap into some of their most valued practical tools and techniques. Like them, you can then apply these immediately to make a real difference in your performance.

This is your personal, practical pocket book. Here you can take your own and others' wisdom and learning and transform it into actions for you, in both work and life.

Profits from this book go to our Charity – the Inspiring Leadership Trust – for disadvantaged women and children in the UK and internationally. Please visit our charity website for further information if you wish to get involved:

www.inspiringleadershiptrust.com

Using this book

This book is divided into three parts:

How Best to Use This Book

In this pocket book of wisdom there is a wealth of material to absorb, reflect on and apply to your own leadership. It is a very rich meal; it is not advised to consume it in one sitting. To do so would be like trying to drink from a fire hydrant. This is a book that is intended to help you:

1. Jog your memory
2. Dip into for a specific leadership dilemma you are seeking to resolve.
3. As your daily reference book to carry in your pocket or bag with you on your travels.

Other leaders said about this pocket book, "We valued such a short, snappy selection of profound thoughts. On reading each tip we needed to stop, reflect and think about what they mean to our own leadership context."

Overview of Inspiring Leadership

Research shows that IQ accounts for circa only 6% of performance, and EQ around 30%. So, the important question is; what is in the 64% gap?

We have collaborated with Dr. Reuven Bar-On, world renowned psychologist and expert in emotional intelligence to answer the question. Our research shows that the Inspiring Leadership compass directly correlates with more holistic performance and potential. Developing your skills and behaviours in any of the 8 components will make a significant impact on your own and others' lives and that of your organisation.

A few key highlights from our research

We're not fans of gender stereotyping - it's disingenuous to everyone. As soon as this becomes our collective mantra, then we box ourselves in and will fail to reach our full potential or inspire others to think differently. Our judgments, both of ourselves and others, are viewed through a tainted lens fuelled by bias, of which there is enough already!

Instead, aim to build your own self-awareness, play to your strengths and understand the environment in which you are operating in, in a way that will help you succeed.

> "We cannot change what we are not aware of, and once we are aware, we cannot help but change."
>
> *Sheryl Sandberg*

There are however some key insights that came through from our research that are worth noting;

1. There is ZERO significant statistical difference between inspiring male and female leaders. They are all highly adept and even role modelling each of the 8 components of the Inspiring Leadership Compass.

2. There is a significant difference, however, between average and inspiring leaders. The good news is, our brains are highly malleable and, with the right attitude and self-belief, we can develop new skills in order to become

Leigh & Jonathan Bowman-Perks MBE

even more successful.

3. One of the concerning trends in our assessments was that, even when women were independently assessed as high or exceptional performers, they systematically rated themselves lower! Holding limiting self-belief systems or understanding of one's true impact and value has a direct correlation with personal performance and career success.

4. Male and female leaders who were able to be truly authentic, were more happily successful in work and life. For those who were not, there was a direct correlation with elevated stress levels which negatively impacted on physical and mental health and well-being.

Inspiring Leaders' Practical Tips and Tools

We have consolidated the tips under each of the 8 Inspiring Leadership Principles around the compass. We have included an extra topic specifically dedicated to running effective team meetings. This is because, whilst between 60 –80% of leader's time is spent in team meetings, a significant proportion of our team development work is dedicated to addressing ineffective meetings and behaviours. Please use the books as you wish – either from start to finish or dip in anywhere.

Your Personal Action Plan

It's all about transforming your learning into action. Write down your SMART actions (Specific, Measurable, Achievable, Results-orientated and Time-bound). These will help you to create the necessary laser-like focus and absolute commitment in order to be more successful. We have added questions and space for you to add your own learning throughout this pocket book. And remember:

"The only limit to our realisation of tomorrow will be our doubts of today".

Franklin D Roosevelt

Leigh & Jonathan Bowman-Perks MBE

"Our deepest fear is not that we are inadequate. Our deepest fear is that we are powerful beyond measure. It is our light, not our darkness that most frightens us. Your playing small does not serve the world. There is nothing enlightened about shrinking so that other people won't feel insecure around you. We are all meant to shine, as children do... And as we let our own light shine, we unconsciously give other people permission to do the same. As we are liberated from our own fear, our presence automatically liberates others."

Marianne Williamson

About Inspiring Leadership…
it's not about role or title, it is a way of being with others, so they willingly trust and follow you. It is a leadership performance philosophy and mindset based on many years of experience and research.

Inspiring Women Leaders…
breathe life into others through their energy, passion, gravitas, presence, integrity and trustworthiness. They have a strong moral compass, clear sense of what gives their lives meaning and purpose and always consider what will leave a sustainable legacy after they have finished their role. They create a healthy culture through being physically and mentally fit, combined with a robustness and grit to learn from setbacks and adversity. They are humble enough to be willing to learn from coaches, mentors and colleagues. In particular, they use their emotions intelligently so that they work for them as well as reading and managing others well. They have a strong reputation and track record for successfully delivering business performance through the high levels of engagement of others. They are role models to other women in particular

and take personal accountability for helping others to succeed. On the backdrop of a socio-economic meltdown and the growth in hostile activity globally, there has never been a more compelling case for greater diversity and equality. We will not achieve parity for this generation but we can achieve progress; we need to find and craft new solutions fit for 21st century challenges. Remember, ***"a woman's place is in the boardroom"*** and it is now time for inspiring women leaders to embrace the opportunity and fulfilling their full career potential.

Expiring Leaders & Mis-Leaders...
are the polar opposite of Inspiring Women Leaders. Their qualities are grandiosity and exaggerated self-worth, pathological lying, manipulation, lack of remorse, shallowness, and exploitation for financial gain. They leave a trail of disaster and mayhem in their wake. At their best they are ineffectual in both their relationships and work; draining the life energy from others. At their most extreme they are Narcissistic, or even "White Collar Psychopaths". They fail to consider others; it's all about ego, self-advancement and doing whatever it takes to get their way. In their

world of altered reality, white-collar psychopaths believe that their performance and contribution drive success, however, it actually destroys the contribution of their teams and the confidence of individuals around them. At all costs they must be challenged and rooted out from your organisation. Just to reinforce about stereotyping; expiring leadership is not exclusive to either gender. Whilst, there are arguments for and against whether these are learned behaviours or personality traits, one thing is for sure; history has demonstrated that everyone can fall foul, regardless of gender! So, as we navigate the corporate ladder, how can we manage our power and influence with integrity and dignity? ***How can we become Inspiring Women Leaders?***

MQ – MORAL INTEGRITY

MQ – Morals and Integrity

You live life according to a clear set of principles, values and beliefs that guide your decisions, choices and actions. You try to do the right thing at work and in the community. This has been referred to as work ethics, professionalism and moral intelligence.

MQ – Top Tips

"Many CEOs and leaders think that silence is indeed golden, that consensus is bliss. It is – sometimes. But more often what it signifies is that there are no respected processes for surfacing concerns and dissent." *Margaret Heffernan*

1. **Courageous Leadership**
   Having courageous conversations and carrying out courageous acts are the mark of a truly inspiring leader. Consider an inspiring leader who you view as having high integrity and being courageous; what would they do in your situation?

2. **Willful Blindness**
   If you don't challenge dishonesty, lack of integrity and injustice, then you are a bystander. As such you are condoning toxic behaviour. Have the courage to stand by your convictions and do the right thing. Do not be wilfully blind.

3. **What Matters Most?**
   Our lives are often packed with too many

things going on simultaneously. We all have the same number of hours in the day. Choose wisely, according to your values, your top 3 life and top 3 work priorities and build clear boundaries. Then the less important, but necessary things can be built around these "big rocks".

4. **Always Be Where You're Indispensable**
As you continually strive to balance your work and your non-work life, then remember that there are certain events that only you can attend, such as special family moments. Therefore, train up your deputy and delegate more so that you can always be where you're indispensable.

5. **How Much Is Enough?**
Sara Hart asks many astute questions such as, "How will you know when you have enough?" and "If you knew you already had enough, how would you behave then?"

6. **Character vs Environment**
If we make mistakes, then we tend to blame the environment in which we are working, rather than any character defect in ourselves.

However, if somebody else makes a mistake, then we blame it on their character defect and lack of integrity, rather than their challenging environment. Apply wise judgement, yet avoid being judgmental.

7. **The Empty Chair**
When in a one-to-one or team meeting, always have an empty chair to encourage ethical decision-making. This could represent a key absent stakeholder such as your customer, regulator, or other stakeholder. Then you can ask a colleague, "how would you respond to (a person sitting in the empty chair) if they said..."

8. **The Pragmatic Approach To Leadership**
If you are acting with integrity, in a slow, bureaucratic organisation with little empowerment, then you can become overly cautious. Alternatively, take the pragmatic approach to leadership: "It is far better to beg forgiveness afterwards, than to ask permission beforehand!"

9. **Organisational Saboteurs**
Do you have a colleague who is "an

Leigh & Jonathan Bowman-Perks MBE

organizational saboteur?" Do they say, "Yes" to requests and instructions, but then do the complete opposite? Do they deliberately undermine their peers, or boss? Are they cynical, believe they "know it all" and act in a passively aggressive manner? If so, then it is time to help them re-recruit themselves and re-commit to the team, or encourage them to swiftly leave!

10. **If Trust Is Gone, Then They Must Go Too**
    If you don't trust people, you cannot work with them, nor for them. Toxic people affect everyone. If trust is lost and, despite your best efforts, it cannot be rebuilt, then it is time to part company. Always be firm in the decision and kind in the execution when you fire someone.

11. **Be Integrated Not Dis-Integrated**
    When there is congruence and alignment between who you are being, your values and beliefs, the work you are doing and the life you are living, then you are living with integrity. To do otherwise leads you to become dis-integrated, lack authenticity and trustworthiness.

12. **Integrity + Transparency = Trust**
    Inspiring leaders build trusted environments,
    where people feel engaged. This is based
    on their consistently espoused values and
    transparent communication. One of the
    biggest derailers to enabling change is when
    leaders 'protect' people from the truth.
    Treating employees as adults demonstrates
    respect and greater trust.

13. **Trustworthiness**
    The most powerful underlying value that
    defines a leader's success, or failure, is
    whether other people consider them to
    be trustworthy. Steven Covey uses the
    equation Trust = Speed x Cost. When there
    are high levels of trust between people
    then things happen very fast and cheap.
    Otherwise with no or low levels of trust,
    interactions are painfully slow and highly
    expensive.

14. **Authenticity vs Flexibility**
    It's a fine judgement call to move down
    the spectrum from being totally authentic,
    according to your own values and beliefs,
    versus being more culturally flexible to the

norms and culture of the organisation you work in. Find the balance between listening to others' views and sharing your own. Choose your battles carefully and sensitively.

15. **Right And Open-Minded**
Having strong values and principles are essential to inspiring leaders. However, you also need to be pragmatic and realistic to avoid being 'right' but closed to the ideas and perspectives of others. Being stubborn at the wrong moment may be fatal for your leadership.

16. **Play To Your Motivational Drivers**
Work with an expert to complete psychometrics tools that will help you unpick what motivates and drives you, and also what will derail you. These powerful insights will help you to be authentically successful, by providing a deeper self-awareness and sense-check to ensure you are working in a culture that brings out the best in you and in a role that you enjoy, where you are able to work at your best.

Top Tip For Organisations

Inspire From the Top achieving diversity and inclusion needs to be deeply ingrained into the organisational values and culture. *What you do* and *what you say* defines the attitude and culture in your organisation. The problem is not the supply of great female talent, it is demand. For true and sustainable change to happen, the tone needs to be set by the top; not the HR or Diversity Teams but the CEO and their executives. Leaders need to align, take real action and be held to account. Be courageous and stamp out discrimination.

MQ Questions For You

1. What are your top 6 values, beliefs and principles you live your life by?

2. With that in mind what do you need to say, "Yes" to and "No" to more often in your work and life?

3. What courageous conversation or action are you avoiding and why that you need to address?

MQ Your Learning & Action

"When the whole world is SILENT, even one voice becomes POWERFUL"

- Malala Yousafzai

LIVE YOUR LIFE **ON** PURPOSE (RATHER THAN **OFF** PURPOSE)
BY BEING AUTHENTICALLY YOURSELF.

PQ – Meaning and Purpose

You strive to find meaning and purpose in your private life and at work, which leads to a more complete, satisfying and fulfilling life. You are aware of what you perceive to be fundamentally important and meaningful, which goes beyond self-actualisation and personal development to benefit others. You strive to live a life *'on purpose'*, rather than 'off purpose'.

PQ – Top Tips

"I was ordained priest in 1995 (1994 was the first year when women were ordained priests) and I was frequently hearing people say how hard it was for women in those early days because they had no role models. A wise vicar expressed curiosity about why people needed role models as surely this was about becoming fully myself. That has given me great freedom to go on becoming the person God has created me to be." *The Right Revd Rachel Treweek, Bishop of Gloucester*

17. **Living Your Life On Purpose**
    Are you truly "living a life on purpose", rather than "off purpose"? What does it mean to you to have "a life truly well-lived?" Know that you are unique and special. So too all those around you; those you recognise as being like you and those you consider as different. How can you find the courage to go on discovering who you are, build the confidence to be yourself and the humility to learn from others?

18. **Purpose – Why?**
     Many can explain <u>what</u> they do and <u>how</u> they
     do it, but they forget to clarify the powerful
     reason <u>WHY</u>. People will engage when they
     understand and buy into the 'why' you do
     what you do. For example, if the organisers
     of a meeting can't explain its purpose, then
     don't attend.

19. **The Sky's the Limit**
     Don't limit yourself based on your own or
     others' beliefs of what you can or cannot do.
     You will only find out what you are capable of
     if you try to do something you haven't done
     before. Always be authentic to yourself and
     don't be afraid to do something different
     rather than following what's done before or
     what seems safe.

20. **Consider All Career Options**
     With so few women leading in STEM
     (Science, Technology, Engineering and
     Mathematics), government (including peace
     and security) or even non-traditional roles,
     have you thought broadly about your talents,
     experience and potential to bring your
     expertise to bear in such worthwhile key

positions of influence with deep societal and cultural impacts?

21. **"You never fail until you stop trying" (Einstein)**
Sometimes to start trying is the hardest step. It may be daunting and self doubt, but beware of the procrastination that can set in that holds you back. By taking the first few simple steps; you will build your confidence and it will bring success and fulfilment. Believe in yourself!

22. **Balcony vs Dance-Floor**
Get off the dance floor and up onto the balcony. Then you will be able to see the big picture and make your 3 strategic, value-adding decisions for this year. Avoid micromanagement; encourage your reports to have empowered execution to take action themselves. Alternatively, if you are too trapped in your 'ivory tower', get onto the dance-floor and be visible with your employees as a way to listen and engage.

23. **2-Up, 1-Up And My Part In Their Plan**
Always consider the requirements of your boss 2 levels up, 1 level up and your part

in delivering that success. Be clear on what they define as your purpose and success criteria. Capture your boss's Success and Satisfaction criteria on just 1 Page.

24. **Focus**
Check – do you have a personal vision to live your life on purpose? Have you a laser- like focus on what matters and what you are doing that adds true value? Avoid dissipating your energy by spreading yourself too thinly.

25. **Apportion Time According To Your Priorities**
Decide what your ideal week is like and how you should apportion your finite time to achieve your Main Effort and Subsidiary Efforts. Then make a pie chart of how you have actually allocated your time every week. Is it congruent? Are you spending far too much time on things that had little value?

26. **Look Forwards vs In The Rearview Mirror**
Leading strategically is like driving a car. You do need to glance occasionally in the rearview mirror to learn from what has happened in the past; however, 90% of your time should be spent looking forward and

planning.

27. **Drive - The Surprising Truth About What Motivates People**
Daniel Pink highlights that, instead of money, it is autonomy, mastery and purpose that takes people from mere compliance to greater self-direction and commitment to work that matters.

28. **Follow Your Passion/Joy/Love**
Work out what gives you true joy, happiness and produces a resonant vibration within you. This is when you are "in flow" doing what you love doing and performing at the top of your game. When you know what gives you bliss, then follow it. Anything less is a compromise and diminishes your authenticity.

29. **Internally Or Externally Controlled?**
You need to seriously consider whether you are the creator of your life or you are passively responding to it. As the creator, then you are the cause and your life is the effect. When you are passive, then the world is the cause of what happens to you and you

are affected by it. Choose to be the cause and not the effect of your life. Be proactive not reactive - take control; don't just be controlled by external events and people.

30. **Beware Upward Delegation**
If you have a culture where everyone delegates upwards to you, then it's your fault. That's because you've created a lack of trust that prevents your subordinates from being able to think for themselves, get on, feel empowered and make things happen. Stop being a control freak; instead coach and bring on those you lead.

31. **Be Clear On Expectations**
Never assume what someone wants, what they mean or that they understand your expectations either. Clarify and ask questions so you completely understand. To assume means you, or they, might misinterpret and this inevitably leads to wasting time or causing issues further down the road.

32. **Urgent vs Important**
Steven Covey has some great tips. One is "the things which matter most should not be

at the expense of things which matter least!"
A sense of urgency can be addictive and
make us feel powerful and useful, but may
not add value. Be proactive and focus on the
important, not just the urgent aspects of your
role.

33. **The Top 3 Value-Adding Tasks**
As a daily discipline, at the end of the day
capture the top 3 tasks that you should

Leigh & Jonathan Bowman-Perks MBE

perform the next day. These must add the most value to your job. Then first thing in the morning put them in priority order. Then begin with priority 1 and don't give up until you've completed it, before you move onto priority 2 and then onto 3.

34. **Commitment, Or Merely Compliance?**
Check with yourself and those you lead whether they are fully committed to your organisation, the idea, or change proposed, or whether they are just ticking boxes and only complying in a half-hearted way. Tap into what each individual needs to build commitment, rather than making assumptions, or ignoring that you have dissent in the ranks.

35. **Commitment Wake-up Call**
Write a postcard giving yourself 3 pieces of career advice and give it to your coach, colleague or a friend to post to you 3 months later. There is no better reminder to help you take responsibility for your progress on the commitments you make and encourage you to become your own architect.

Top Tip For Organisations

Women influence 80% of purchasing decisions and represent 60% of the graduate population globally. Take time to understand the <u>internal</u> and <u>external</u> context underpinned by facts, to determine 'why' gender balance is so important for your organisation from both a customer and talent perspective. Find and craft new solutions that are fit for 21st century leadership issues. Address the systems, processes, policies and culture that are holding you back. It is the route to attracting and retaining more diverse talent and gaining competitive advantage.

PQ Questions For You

1. What gives your life and your work meaning
and purpose?

2. What do you need to say 'no' to in order to
say 'yes' to something else?

3. According to Mark Twain's quote – have
you yet found out why you were born?

PQ Your Learning & Action

"The most difficult thing is the decision to act, the rest is merely tenacity."
    - Amelia Earhart

BE A CORPORATE ATHLETE. CHANGE YOURSELF AND
DON'T WALLOW IN A TOXIC CULTURE.

HQ – Health and Well-Being

You strive to achieve and maintain good physical and emotional health, which leads to a sense of overall well-being. You keep physically fit, emotionally balanced, energetic and productive. If you are a healthy leader then you are infectious and inspire others, who are typically attracted to you and express a desire to work with and for you.

HQ

Role Archetype: Healthy Energiser

Wellbeing · Self-Belief · Emotions Management · HEALTH · Self-Management · PHYSICAL FITNESS · BALANCE · Positive · Attitude · CULTURE · Nutrition

HQ – Top Tips

"Individuals working in corporate environments
are exposed to high levels of uncertainty and
change. Everything from pressure, competitiveness,
exposure, volatility, hyper-busyness, team
management or bad leadership can create fear
and vulnerability. This critical issue is having
a detrimental impact on individual health and
energy, and inevitably organisational wellbeing
and performance, which needs recognition and
intervention." *Nathan Newton-Willington, Personal
Trainer and Nutrition Coach*

36. **Your Personal And Organisational Health**
    You need your organisation to be lean, fit,
    resilient and dynamic. It follows that, as a
    leader, you need to be the same. What can
    you do to significantly increase your personal
    energy and vitality?"

37. **Do something about it!**
    Adopt John F. Kennedy's wise saying
    embodied by Amnesty International, "better
    to light a candle than to curse the darkness."

Take action rather than criticise.

38. **Let Go of Resentment**
Take heed of Nelson Mandela's saying:
"Resentment is like drinking poison and
then hoping it will kill your enemies." And
the other saying, "Resentment is like letting
someone you dislike live rent free in your
head."

39. **10-10-10 Perspective**
You need to get the perspective of time,
especially when you are so deep in
the problem that you "cannot see the wood
for the trees". Ask yourself, "How important
will this problem be firstly in 10 hours time,
then in 10 months time and ultimately in 10
years time?"

40. **Words Create Worlds**
Take care over what you say; it will
subliminally shape the way you think and
behave. As Henry Ford said, "Whether you
think you can, or whether you think you
can't, you're probably right!" Your attitude
will define your altitude.

41. **Relative Deprivation**
Be careful about constantly comparing yourself to other leaders and groups, putting them on a pedestal. Giving increased status to others relative to yourself can be unhealthy, demoralising and may erode your confidence. Value your own strengths and talents, rather than making everything relevant to what others have.

42. **Your Physiology Shapes Your Leadership Impact**
Make connections with others to generate the hormone oxytocin. Keeping fit and healthy will also generate endorphins, dopamine and serotonin. Work on staying calm and adopt a positive mental attitude to generate DHEA, the vitality hormone. Negative emotions and thoughts will generate Cortisol, the stress hormone.

43. **Eagles Or Turkeys?**
Do you help your team members soar like eagles - in their own patch of clear blue sky and returning to the communal nest at the end of the day? Or do you treat them like turkeys - stuck under the spotlight in everyone else's ammonia, packed together,

Leigh & Jonathan Bowman-Perks MBE

with no room to breathe or move in your barn? Empowering your team creates a healthy environment.

44. **Go Easy On Yourself**
Perfectionists are highly self-critical. The problem is that you then hold other people to the same exacting standards and are more critical of people around you. Look for the good in others, catch them doing things right. Don't over-estimate what you can achieve by trying to do it all perfectly; instead be kind to yourself and accept when something is good enough. Rather than constantly striving and doing, just be present with them more often. Create more time to think and re-gather your resources ready for the next big challenge.

45. **Laughter Is The Best Medicine**
Don't take yourself too seriously; no one else does! Ask yourself "does this bring joy, love and happiness to my life and am I having fun?" If the answer is no, then stop doing it! You always have a choice; focus more on what you love and your unique talents.

46. **What Is Your Healthiest Calling/ Job?**

What really should you be doing as the healthiest job for yourself? The inner circle of the Inspiring Leadership Compass, shows the energy and balance given to: (1) Myself; (2) My Relationships; (3) My Organisation and; (4) My Society. Draw the circle and for each write; words that capture your passions, what success looks like, what you want to protect then reflect on what is and isn't working. Now, identify what you need to say 'no' and 'yes' to. By creating clear boundaries, you are able to build greater balance in all aspects of work and life.

47. **You're In The Energy Business**

As an inspiring Leader, you need to energise and inspire yourself first, before you can energise anyone else to willingly follow

Leigh & Jonathan Bowman-Perks MBE

you, or be influenced by you. They in turn will give 20-30% more discretionary life energy to the organisation and most importantly your customers, who will consequently come back for repeat business.

48. **Ratio: Done To Me vs Done By Me**
It is far healthier (mentally) when you have control of your own life and destiny, rather than have things being done to you without you being able to stop or influence them. Equally, the same is true for the people you lead: give them more autonomy.

49. **White Collar Psychopaths & Toxic Leaders**
Toxic leaders hide their vulnerability, fail to have open and honest conversations with you, cannot be trusted, or relied upon and are dysfunctional. Beware of their cold, rather than warm, empathy and lack of genuine emotional connection with you. You are not able to change their behaviour, so insulate and protect yourself from them. Record and evidence all your interactions. Be courageous, act with integrity and get them out of the organisation.

50. **F.E.A.R.**
= Forget Everything And Run OR Face
Everything And Rise! Between the external
stimuli and your own internal response,
remember you have choice. Pause, take a
few deep breaths to regulate your body and
then plan how you will respond in order to
'rise'.

51. **Toxic Teams**
Toxic, dysfunctional teams lack a sense of
purpose, direction, loyalty, or values. In the
absence of good leadership, they fall back
on criticising everyone else, failing to accept
personal responsibility, undermining their
colleagues and wallowing in gossip. The
antidote is to provide clarity, direction and
accountability that models collaboration
and healthy behaviours. Identify and remove
the 'bad apples' that corrupt others and
undermine the performance of the business.

52. **Sleeping Beauty**
Don't stay up too late on a school night;
every bit of anything good that happens
inside your body such as learning, repairing
and healing is done while you sleep, so make

sure you try to get at least 7 hours.

53. **Rewire Your Brain for Success**
Our friend the psychologist Marisa Peer in her TEDx talk said, "First you make your beliefs, then your beliefs make you. Make the unfamiliar familiar and the familiar unfamiliar. Choose to link pleasure to the things you want and pain to being stuck in an unhealthy behaviour/place."

54. **Put Your Own Oxygen Mask on First**
Then Help Others You cannot be there for others if you don't take care of yourself first. Take time out every day to 'power down'. Sit still in silence, with no devices - phone, tv, computer - and just breathe. This is especially powerful at the end of your work day to allow you to leave your work stresses behind and recharge so that you can enjoy your personal time.

55. **The Vending Machine Is The Enemy!**
A diet of caffeine and sugary snacks is a diet starved of nutrients required for effective cognitive function. When we are tired or stressed, the immediate dopamine hit that

we get gives immediate renewed energy, but this is the illusion for the delusional and is addictive! Break bad habits by starting your day as you mean to go on and choosing healthy alternatives.

Where are you on the stress scales?

56. **Step On the Stress Scales!**
Too much Certainty – Yes you can have too much certainty, which can create stagnation and feel draining. It means your mind is under-utilised which can be dangerous to your mental health and leaves a breeding ground for lack of self-worth and depression.

Too much Uncertainty – Uncertainty can be just as harmful as certainty. Too much

Leigh & Jonathan Bowman-Perks MBE

and you can feel emotionally and mentally vulnerable. It can cause procrastination in fear of 'doing it wrong', which can result in you making emotionally based decisions about your career, relationships and health. It is the breeding ground for anxiety.

<u>Just right</u> – The best place is right in the middle. A mild level of uncertainty helps creativity and learning; it will drive you forward. This is coupled with having enough certainty to trust yourself, know you are on the right path and give yourself mental breaks that you need.

57. **Watch out for the Amygdala Hijack!**
Leaders often suffer with their physical health as the environment they work in has a lot more uncertainty and stress than most. This can make every day a fight which means Amygdala (your 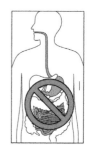 threat response centre) is a lot more active. Once activated, your digestive system turns

OFF. Your body thinks you are about to fight or run. This ancient response doesn't understand the modern world we live in and can't differentiate. You will bloat, struggle to eat whole meals throughout the day because they are not digested, crave sugar and caffeine because the nutrients from the undigested food can not be absorbed and the cycle repeats daily.

58. **Eat Move Sleep**
Tom Rath advises how small choices in how you exercise, eat and sleep lead to big changes in your life. You will have far more energy for work and non-work elements of your life.

59. **Imposter Syndrome Banished!**
A concept more prevalent in women, particularly who are high achieving. If you stay true to your values, commit to your authentic self, and create purpose, you then need to start to accepting your accomplishments and challenge your inner dialogue that tells you that you are not enough!

Leigh & Jonathan Bowman-Perks MBE

Top Tip For Organisations

You don't need a million tick box initiatives to drive change. The inevitable hyper-busyness of multiple diversity activities has become our default and narrative for action being taken. Often, they are superficial and now proven to be what we call a WOMBAT - Waste Of Money, Bandwidth and Time! Address the deep cultural and structural issues that hold you back from retaining and promoting their female talent. Focus on the top 3 initiatives that will drive the greatest change, and embed them within the organisation.

HQ Questions For You

1. In what ways can you become physically and mentally healthier?

2. Is your work environment healthy or toxic and what are your going to do about it and the toxic people you may work with?

HQ Your Learning & Action

"Women in particular need to keep an eye on their physical health... We need to do a better job of putting ourselves higher on the 'to do' list."

- Michelle Obama

IQ – WISDOM AND JUDGEMENT

CREATE STRATEGIC THINKING TIME IN ORDER
TO MAKE BETTER DECISIONS

IQ – Cognitive Intelligence and Wisdom

You have the ability to learn new things, apply learned knowledge, solve problems and make good decisions based on sound judgment and wisdom. Your good decisions and choices incorporate a reasonable course of action combined with past experience, learning from others wisdom and what has worked and openness to learning new things that could work to attain your desired results. You are wise in addition to being *intelligent.*

IQ

Role Archetype: Trusted Advisor

Thinking Environment

Wisdom Decisive Talents Development

LEARNING

Experienced CURIOUS Mentor Creative Solution-Oriented

Coach

Reflective

IQ – Top Tips

"I believe that success is not a zero sum game. You need to build your team and share successes with them. Strong leadership is the expression of a coalition of values. Building consensus creates a position of strength. Don't be surprised at the loneliness of leadership and believe in who you are. You need to press 'delete' on the imposter syndrome button."
Rt Hon Dame Tessa Jowell MP DBE

60. **Be The Architect Of Your Own Destiny**
    If you don't ask the answer will always be no. Opportunities come along when you least expect. Always be open minded and prepared to give something new a try. Ask for that promotion you really deserve. Volunteer to lead a project that you're really passionate about. Be curious and try new things – preferably outside your comfort zone! Learn to say 'yes' and find the reasons why you should stretch yourself.

61. **Generate Your Own Wisdom Team**
Gather around you your own virtual and real team of experts and advisers; your wisdom team. Accumulate your own coach, mentors, friends and advisors; people whom you can turn to in order to help your own finest thinking and decision-making.

62. **Giants Not Dwarfs**
Surround yourself with a truly high performing team. Recruit and develop a metaphorical army of giants - people who (in their own specialist areas) are bigger and taller then you and far more talented. You can then have time to really think at the strategic level, be on the balcony, and make yourself available for promotion on to even more demanding roles. Sadly, too many people surround themselves with metaphorical dwarfs, who are less talented than them and pose no threat, or challenge.

63. **Build Self Awareness**
Johari's window technique is to help you achieve a better understanding of yourself and your impact, by uncovering what is know and unknown to you and others.

The use of tools such as 360o feedback and psychometrics can help further your awareness by making the unconscious conscious. This helps you to focus your energy on the development areas that will make the greatest impact to your performance.

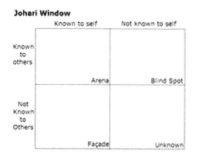

Johari Window

	Known to self	Not known to self
Known to others	Arena	Blind Spot
Not Known to Others	Façade	Unknown

64. **Monkeys**

People bring you problems – metaphorical monkeys on their backs. Their aim is to transfer these monkeys onto your back, or leave them in your office, and then get away quickly. Take a Coach-Approach to Leadership by asking them great questions, so they keep their own monkeys and take away one of yours too.

65. **Sharpen The Saw**
Stephen Covey tells the famous story of a
man in a wood sawing through a large tree.
You ask him, "how long have you been doing
that?" to which he replies, "3 hours and it is
such hard work! I may never get this job
done!" You then ask him, "Why don't you
stop and sharpen the saw? To which he
replies, "Can't you see, stupid? - I haven't
got time - I'm too busy sawing through the
tree!"

66. **40 Days To Embed Behavioural Change**
Neuroscientists, like our friend Dr Jeff Bird,
know that it takes 40+ days of continual
practice to embed a change in leadership
behaviour. Like going to the gym - 1 session
never sustains the change.

67. **Your Best Friend**
When you have a deeply personal problem
that is keeping you awake at night, try taking
the perspective of someone you trust, such
as your best friend. Imagine that your best
friend has exactly the same problem as you

Leigh & Jonathan Bowman-Perks MBE

have now. Then write down what advice you would give your best friend. Now take that good advice yourself.

68. **Living Above The 45°** When you live on diagonal 45° line, then your abilities match your challenges exactly - that is a comparatively easy and comfortable place. If, however, you live above the 45° then you will find you are stretched and challenged. This is in a state of unknown can be both in the space of fear and vulnerability, of not knowing, of potentially being wrong and exciting, because of the new opportunity. Embrace your full potential.

69.   **The One Log In The Logjam**
Picture this image and metaphor. When
Canadian timber firms send their huge logs
speeding down the fast owing rivers, on their
way to the sawmills, they can pile-up on
sharp bends. The job of 1 specialist 'log-jam
person' is to identify the critical 1 log in a pile
of up to 200, then re a harpoon into it and
rapidly winch it out, in order to let the whole
logjam race on again down the river. Do the
same with your problems.

70.   **Listen To Your Head, Heart, Gut And Purse**
We have 89 Billion neurons in our brain,
40,000 in our Heart and 100 Million in our
Gut (mini brains). Listen to your head, heart,
gut and purse (finances) and keep tuned into
your instinct for being alert to deceit, danger
and "things that seem too good to be true" –
they nearly always are too good and not true!

71.   **Positive vs Negative Commands**
The human mind responds best to clear
commands. Tell your brain what you want
(your self talk), not what you don't want. It
has problems with negatives and losing
things. For example, telling a child, "don't

touch the hot stove" – they don't hear the negative part of your command and still touch it. To get fitter, give yourself a target weight, rather than saying 'lose X weight'.

72. **Pre-Mortem - Scenario Planning**
Imagine you are 12 months down the line and the plan you have just come up with has fundamentally failed. Do a pre-mortem: What was it that you did that went wrong? Now plan strategies to mitigate those risks, before they are likely to emerge.

73. **Results Only Work Environment (ROWE)**
Focus on the results of the people you lead, rather than presenteeism, attending meetings and clocking-in and clocking-out of a set work environment. Give them 20% of their weekly time to develop new ideas, which add true value to your organisation beyond their day-to-day jobs.

74. **KISS = Keep It Simple Stupid**
To paraphrase Albert Einstein, "Everything should be as simple as possible, but no simpler." Inspiring leaders make the complex clearer, simpler and easier for everyone

to understand and act upon. Philosopher Henry David Thoreau said, "Simplify, simplify, simplify", to which Ralph Waldo Emerson replied, "I think 1 would have sufficed!"

75. **10,000 Hours / 10 Years**
You are not born with talent; it comes from hard work. Research shows you need to give 10,000 hours of purposeful practice into your profession to become an expert. When you see someone who is the best at what they do, just know they are being rewarded in public for the many times they have practiced in private.

76. **Listen & Learn From Others**
A wise piece of advice, "Everyone has something to teach you; if only you would truly listen to them."

77. **Open And Closed Loops**
Un-cram your RAM. A bit like a computer, your brain's Random Access Memory (RAM) quickly fills up. Then, when you have too many "open loops" you cannot think particularly well. This is especially the case at night, when the brain goes through its

Leigh & Jonathan Bowman-Perks MBE

cleaning, learning and sorting process. So quickly write down the next action step you must take and "close the loop". Then you can move on to the next activity in the daytime, or go back to more restful sleep at night.

78. **Don't try and sleep through the worrying thought**
This problem of "open loops" is especially true when you are stressed and anxious in the middle of the night and are woken worrying about something. Have a small torch, pen and pad of paper by the bed. When you wake worrying, then write the action down and go back to sleep – it will still be there in the morning.

79. **Combine Career Breaks/Maternity Leave And Development**
Contrary to popular belief, they are not diametrically opposed. By engaging in projects, community activities and personal development whilst on career breaks or maternity leave is a great way to keep intellectually stimulated, passionate about a broader purpose, as well as helps with confidence.

Top Tip For Organisations

Make Female Talent More Visible Avoid goals
which point to tokenism, and instead create
a culture of meritocracy; remember, there is
more than enough female talent out there! Pair
talented women with senior male executives
for a reciprocal mentoring programme. Women
receive senior executive visibility, advice and
opportunities, and the senior executive also
widen their views on women across the business
and heard first hand some of the barriers or
concerns which they were previously unaware
of. Place a lens on critical decision points
where people decisions are made: reward;
development; promotions; talent reviews;
recruitment; return to work programmes etc.

Leigh & Jonathan Bowman-Perks MBE

IQ Questions For You

1. How can you create more time to think?

2. How can you make better decisions?

3. How can you stretch yourself and live above the 45 degree line to really learn and grow?

IQ Your Learning & Action

"There's a special place in hell for women who do not help other women."

- Madeleine Albright

EQ—EMOTIONAL AND SOCIAL INTELLIGENCE

USE YOUR EMOTIONS INTELLIGENTLY. BUILD TRUST AND RAPPORT SO PEOPLE WILLINGLY WORK FOR YOU.

EQ – Top Tips

You are: (1) aware of and understand emotions as well as effectively express feelings, (2) understand how others feel and relate well with them, (3) manage and control your emotions to cope with daily demands, problems and pressure, (4) manage change, adapt and solve personal and interpersonal problems, as well as (5) generate positive mood and are sufficiently self-motivated and fully engaged. Some refer to this as *emotional intelligence*.

80. **Listen Without Needing To Be Right**
Much of the time we are not truly listening
to other people because of our prejudices
and negative judgement. Practise listening to
other people without needing to be right; it
will truly allow you and them to do your finest
thinking.

81. **Invest In Your Emotional Bank Accounts**
It pays to invest relationship energy in your
various stakeholders; don't just transact.
Rather, top up your emotional bank accounts
with each of them by building rapport
and trust. Then when you call on them for
support you have something to draw on.

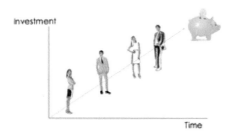

82. **WIIFM & WAMI**
In a meeting always consider everyone else

Leigh & Jonathan Bowman-Perks MBE

present and their perspectives from the point of view of, "What's In It For Me (WIIFM)?" and "What's Against My Interests (WAMI)?"

83. **Assumptions**
Ask, "What are we/am I assuming that is stopping us/me progressing?" Consider the "un-true limiting assumptions that you are living as if they are true".

84. **WWW**
Always begin any meeting asking the question, "What is Working Well (WWW) in your work/personal life?" This technique is used in reviews and personal appraisals. You can also end any meeting asking, "What Worked Well in this meeting?"

85. **EBI**
If you're looking to improve situations, where things are not going well, you should ask, "What would make it Even Better If (EBI) we did it?" In that way people are looking for solutions to problems, rather than just complaining about problems.

86. **Be In The Room**
The power of being truly present with someone, by listening to them and being very attentive of what they think, say and do, is significant. So when you are in the room, be IN the room. Don't be on your mobile, or mentally still in the last meeting, or worrying about the next meeting.

87. **Non-Violent Communications (NVC)**
When faced with emotionally charged, conflict situations, try the NVC approach of Marshall Rosenberg. Capture the 4 FFCR steps: Facts, Feelings, Consequences and my Request.

88. **"Yes And" Rather Than "Yes But"**
If you use a sentence such as, "You've done a great job, but there were some problems …" Then do not be surprised if people forget everything before the BUT and just remember the criticism that follows it. Is far more powerful to say "You've done a great job <u>and</u> what will make it even better would be if…"

89. **Clear Boundaries & Clear Rules Of Engagement**
The greatest misunderstandings and problems are caused by a lack of clarity in meetings and relationships. Be explicit about your expectations from both sides, what your boundaries are and your rules of engagement/ground rules for how your team will work most effectively together.

90. **Less Is More - Churchill's 1-Page**
Mark Twain apologised, "I am sorry this is a long letter, if I had spent more time, I would have written you a short one." Churchill concurred and always insisted on 1-page briefs. Keep your talks to 3 points. Less is more.

91. **Talk More – Email Less**
There is some crucial email etiquette, to save you and others time. Speak to people rather than emailing them. Never blind copy (Bcc) - it "always ends in tears", because you should have been more honest in the first place. People ultimately get to see Bcc email copies that you didn't want them to see.

92. **Appreciation - Catching People Doing Things <u>Right</u>**
Too many leaders are hypercritical: always pointing out what you are doing wrong. Change that by catching people doing things right and say specifically what you appreciate and value about them. Use 3 x Ss - be Specific, Succinct and Sincere.

93. **White Space**
Your job as the leader is to listen at a deep level and understand the white space between the words, the gaps between silos and team members, in order to understand what's missing and needs to be questioned, or added.

94. **From C2 To "Me Too!"**
Many organisations still prefer a bureaucratic, hierarchical, command and control (C2) structure, with which to run their business. This is an intimidation-based, only good news, fear-of-failure culture. Through coaching, mentoring, empowerment and delegation, inspire your colleagues with powerful stories. Then they will connect with you and your stories, say "me too!" and willingly choose to follow you.

Leigh & Jonathan Bowman-Perks MBE

95. **Be A Story Teller**
The power of storytelling is immense.
Touch people's emotions, make it personal,
share your own story and your vulnerability.
Underpin your stories with meaning, values
and a clear moral to the story. Powerful
Stories = Data + Soul.

96. **Be Empathetic, Whilst Knowing When To Act**
The power of emotional intelligence should
never be underestimated; using your
empathy to read others is crucial. So too is
the sense of judgement to know when you
have to make tough, unpopular decisions
and personally take command, in order to
get stalled teams moving forward against
tough opposition.

97. **Stimulus & Response**
Between being emotionally triggered
(stimulated) by somebody treating you in a
specific way and responding to them, you
always have choice. Never forget that; you
can choose how you manage your reactions.
Use your power; don't give it away.

98. **Acceptance To Let Go**
    The stoic philosophy has some useful
    advice. One is that when you have had a bad
    experience act as if you choose it and then
    you can live with it. Let go of your irritation
    and move on in your life.

99. **Vary Channels to improve two-way communication
    across the business**
    Start doing a weekly internal blog – informal
    and illustrated with photos of great things
    happening in the business. Invite 'guest'
    bloggers to tell stories – a real mix of people
    from right across the business from the most
    junior to more senior and from new starters
    to the better known. Great stories and
    storytellers will engage, enthuse and inspire
    the business.

100. **Invest in a Five Minute Journal**
    Right at the start of the day jot down three
    things you're grateful for and three things
    that would make the day great. Then at the
    end of the day you reflect on what's gone
    well and what would have made it even
    better. It helps change the way in which you
    start the day and focuses you on what really

Leigh & Jonathan Bowman-Perks MBE

matters.

101. **Disagree Well**
There will always be differences of opinion,
debates and arguments; it is important
to handle these potential high conflict
conversations well and not take them
personally. Ensure you act with composure,
graciousness and dignity. It creates the
foundation for trust, gravitas and a strong
reputation when you do not lose your head,
when all around you there may be people
losing theirs!

102. **Givers and Takers**
Giving abundantly to everything and
everyone, may provide the 'Giver' with the
positive stroke they need, but it is draining
and impedes performance. Be careful of
taking on other people's monkeys - you
know, the tasks or even guilt trips that others
want to offload. Learn the art of saying 'no'
before you find you're running a zoo! Equally,
start asking more for what you need! You
may not want to ask for fear of burdening
people, or seeming incompetent, however,
75% to 95% of giving in organisations starts

with an 'Ask'!

103. **Five Minute Favours**
We must give selflessly to help other women
more, and with no expectation of anything in
return. This is the philosophy of abundance,
a belief where there is endless opportunity
for all, and not scarcity. Trust in karma and
do make sure you do a five-minute favour for
someone else each day.

Leigh & Jonathan Bowman-Perks MBE

Top Tip For Organisations

Knowledge is Key to Diversity Awareness In order to engage both men and women, you will need to communicate in a way that resonates with 100% of the talent and customers. This can only be achieved through deeper understanding and awareness of cultures and stereotypes. Create meaningful interventions that invite everyone to the room on leadership topics; women's programmes will always be limited when half the leadership who should be in the room are actually excluded!

EQ Questions For You

1. How can you use your emotions more intelligently?

2. Who can you seek out as a peer or direct report and then appreciate qualities about them and their work?

3. How can you become even more inspiring in your communications and relationships?

Leigh & Jonathan Bowman-Perks MBE

EQ Your Learning & Action

"The greatest human craving is to be appreciated. I believe you have not lived the perfect day until you do something for someone who cannot repay you."

- Pinky Lilani

BE RESILIENT TO ADVERSITY AND LEARN FROM IT.

RQ – Resilience

This is your ability to successfully cope with disappointment, crisis and catastrophe, as well as the ability to recover from these setbacks and learn from them. You often become wiser and more resilient than before from these crucible moments. It is your ability to bounce back from adversity and thriving rather than merely surviving.

RQ
Role Archetype: Resource Mobiliser
WILLPOWER
Successful
Adaptable
RESILIENCE
Vulnerable
Resourceful
Celebration
Perspective
ACTION-ORIENTED

RQ – Top Tips

"There's a saying, behind every man there is
a successful woman. It's the same for women
leaders. You need a great relationship where your
partner is encouraging you to succeed. It makes a
huge difference to my career. It kept me sane!"
Dame Anne Pringle

104. **Mistakes, Learning & Action**
"Mistakes are inevitable; learning from that
experience is optional". Whenever something
doesn't work out as you planned, rather than
beat yourself up, reflect and ask yourself the
question, "What have I learnt and now what
can I do differently to be more successful?"

105. **Do Or Do Not – There Is No "Try"**
"Do or Do Not – there is no Try" - this is the
famous response in the film Star Wars from
the wise Yoda when Luke Skywalker says
he will "give it a try" when doubting his own
abilities in the face of huge challenges and
adversity.

106. **I Like Fear – Fear Sets Me Free!**
Consider this 3-step process: Step 1: Turn and face your own fears - say to yourself, "Bring it on!" Step 2: say "I like fear" Step 3: say "Because fear sets me free!" With such a healthy attitude you realise that your fears and anxieties are just assumptions. They need to be challenged to evaporate and let you get on with doing your real job.

107. **Face Challenges With A Sense of Adventure**
The book We're Going On A Bear Hunt (Michael Rosen) describes a family adventure filled with obstacles. There are no easy paths, but the trickier ones are certainly more enlightening and the more challenges, the less fear; and so the adventure begins! So take a deep breath, face your fears and be adventurous! What is the worst that can happen?

108. **Your Motivation: Towards Or Away From?**
Some people are motivated by fear and getting away from something painful that they don't like. Others are motivated by attraction for an exciting future that they are moving towards. When applying for new

jobs, or trying to inspire other people, then be aware that language related to 'towards' is far more energising and attractive to others.

109. **If We Do Nothing Else We Must...**
It is crucial to decide the purpose of every meeting and that the decision, actions and next steps are agreed at the end. Otherwise, you are wasting your day. To be really focused ask out loud, "If we do nothing else then we must..." Get them to fill in the blank.

110. **Oscillate Between High Performance & Energy Renewal**
Much as you would like to, you cannot be always on and working at top speed and full power. You must find times to replenish and renew your energy sources, both physically and mentally, through giving yourself downtime. This is especially true of having sufficient sleep - ideally 8 hours 36 minutes for the most successful high-performance.

111. **Change Overload & Change Weariness**
Too much continuous change overloads us all, we become weary and very little gets

successfully implemented to stand the test of time and be sufficiently sustainable. Take sufficient holidays and completely switch off from work; read, sleep a lot, relax, do activities and refresh yourself physically and mentally for the challenges when you come back to work.

112. **Positive Attitude To Change**
Winston Churchill had 3 memorable quotes with regards to change: "When confronted by change, it is better to take it by the hand; if you don't it will take you by the throat!" "Change is inevitable; resistance is futile". When criticised for changing his opinion on a very complex situation he replied, "When the situation changes, then I change my opinion. What do you do?"

113. **Speed To Recovery**
As all athletes know, especially business athletes, the fitter you are, then the quicker you recover from intense activity. This is shown most clearly in how quickly you can get your pulse to return to resting heart rate from maximum heart rate.

114. **What Doesn't Kill You, Makes You Stronger**
When you've had a setback, or disappointment, then you need to quickly bounce back mentally and physically. Ask yourself "What is my learning from this failure, setback, or disappointment?" also ask yourself "What was my part in this failure?" Then take action to redress it.

115. **White-Collar Psychopaths & Sociopaths**
Sadly you will occasionally meet white-collar sociopaths/psychopaths. You need huge resilience in order to not be destroyed by them. First remember you cannot change their toxic behaviour - you will break yourself psychologically trying to do so. They have cold empathy, but no warm empathy and completely lack remorse for their devious ways, lying, distortion and use of other people to achieve their own ends. Keep a record of everything and never expect them to be logical. Do not be a bystander to their toxic and deceitful behaviour and do everything you can to expose them and root them out quickly

116. **Don't Accept Damaging Criticism**
It is crucial to learn from feedback. However, if people try and drag you down with damaging and personally nasty criticism, remember "feedback" is a gift and if you don't accept it, then it goes back to them; it's THEIR stuff. Sometimes people try and drag you down in order to lift themselves up. Let them keep it and don't own it.

117. **Relax Into Innovation And Success**
Anxious struggling doesn't work. When you are at your most peaceful, calm and relaxed you will and that your best ideas and innovation come to you. You calm your mind, think positively and so generate the vitality hormone DHEA, rather than the stress hormone Cortisol. It is physically and mentally healthier and leads to success.

118. **High Tempo**
The most successful Organisational Leaders have a high tempo-they can maintain momentum, when switching from one direction to a completely new strategic direction. High tempo requires agile, high performing teams to follow such leaders.

119. **Achieve An Early Win**
Nothing breeds more success like success does. We all like to be on a winning team; it's highly attractive. Set out to achieve small, quick wins to build up confidence and then get bold in your aspirations. Your team will believe they can win again.

120. **Over-Achievers**
If you are an over-achiever, then be prepared to take smaller steps. Then you will build a more resilient, robust and sustainable future. Nature proves that the strongest Hardwood trees put down the deepest roots and grow the most slowly. They can then survive the strongest storms. Trees with shallow roots are blown over and destroyed very quickly. Consequently clarify your MQ, PQ and LQ: be absolutely clear on your values, life meaning and purpose in the legacy you will be leaving.

121. **Be Resilient, Without Being Stupid**
As we will discuss later in the section on RQ, it is important to cope well with adversity, setbacks and disappointment, and have a high level of resilience. However, it is

essential to know when it's time to replenish, renew, refresh and rest. If you do not learn how to self-manage and limit yourself, then it will disastrously affect your health and well-being.

122. **From Surviving To Thriving**
Step beyond merely surviving and adopt an attitude of thriving in the environment of change, entrepreneurship and tough decision-making.

123. **Rules Of Resilience**
With special thanks to our friend Jonathan White, an Ex Royal Marine Officer, who was caught in an IED blast in Afghanistan and became a triple amputee. Now a motivational speaker, he describes The 3 military rules of Resilience: (1) Keep going (2) Keep calm (3) Shit happens, then if rule 3 applies refer back to rule 1!

124. **Believe In Yourself**
It's within your gift and there will always be naysayers out there. If you set your goal to be popular and liked by everyone, then this is misguided. The naysayers can be seen as

the challengers that provide you with the gift of insight. The wonderful thing about a gift is, you can choose not to accept it!

125. **Make the Unfamiliar Familiar**
Avoiding the unfamiliar as it seems too difficult or scary, means that you are avoiding the opportunity to grow and reach your full potential. Like Isabelle Santoire, professional Mountain Guide shared, to get to the top of Everest, you will feel overwhelmed if you only look at the peak. Instead, you need to plan and then take it step by step. Also, spot when the conditions for continuing are perilous and you need to turn back!

"The art of progress is to preserve order amid change and to preserve change amid order"
Alfred North Whitehead

RQ Questions For You

1. How can you show the humility to admit when you need help and don't know the answer?

2. What are the important things that you are avoiding and why? What steps can you take to move forward?

3. What can you do to recharge and renew more often and not get so depleted that you are overwhelmed by your problems?

Leigh & Jonathan Bowman-Perks MBE

RQ Your Learning & Action

"Step out of the history
that is holding you back.
Step into the new story you
are willing to create."
- Oprah Winfrey

BQ - BRAND REPUTATION AND IMPACT

WHAT'S YOUR PERSONAL BRAND, REPUTATION AND IMAGE?

BQ - Brand Presence and Impact

Your *brand* directly reflects the reputation, image and impact that you have developed over time. This is based on the quality of the work you do, on the impact that you make on others, and on what one contributes to the workplace, community and society. It is your trustworthiness and what others say about you when you are not in the room.

BQ

Role Archetype: Brand Promoter

INFLUENCE
Track Record
Brand Alignment
PRESENCE
Visible
Win:Win Oriented
Reputation
Ambassador
NETWORKS
Authentic
Trusted
Politically Savvy

BQ – Top Tips

"You don't have to stay in the 'mould', you can do things your own way. You really have to be yourself, there's nothing more important. I don't have a huge voice for example, so I have to know this and found other ways to adapt."
Lady Susan Rice CBE

126. **Find Both A Mentor <u>And</u> A Sponsor**
Mentors provide a superb opportunity to coach and support you as part of your personal development. A Sponsor has a different role; they are your advocate, someone who will speak up on your behalf and will help you to achieve your potential. If there is not a sponsor programme in your organisation, then create one! It's a great way to get more visibility of the female talent across the organisation and enables more robust execution of talent and development strategies.

127. **Purpose, Plan and Promote (the 3 Ps!)**
To get ahead only putting your head down and working hard – whether it be

for a promotion, a pay rise, a new job – is usually never enough to get achieve your full potential and career success. Women generally feel less comfortable with 'self' promotion, however, you need to know who to influence so see it more as purposeful relationship-building! You need to create <u>plan</u> linked to a clear <u>purpose</u> and then <u>promote</u> yourself in a way that works for you.

128. **Stakeholder Mapping**
Take time to map out a strategy of the people who have power and influence in your organisation and over your career. Then assess your level of visibility and quality of relationship with them. Capture one sheet of how things are now (As Is) and a separate one of the ideal state you would like to move to (To Be) and the actions you need to get there.

129. **Celebrate Your Voice**
A key issue to address is demeanour. Sitting upright, hands on the table flat in front of you, shows that you are calm, alert, listening and interested gives that air of confidence. Be 80% sure of your subject

Leigh & Jonathan Bowman-Perks MBE

matter (you'll never be 100%!) and then have the confidence to voice your opinion in a clear and clam manner. Think about you, but don't over-think as you will miss your moment! Be present and listen to other members of the meeting, as this will help to build your confidence. Set yourself goals of how many times you are going to input in to a meeting before you enter and build this up over time.

130. **How Do You Want Others To Feel?**
Always remember –"People will forget what you say, they will forget what you did, but they will never, never forget how you made them feel!" Think ahead to forthcoming meetings and be aware of the impact of your presence and behaviour on how you will make other people feel, especially if you violate their dignity.

131. **Image: 1st Impressions**
A series of experiments by Princeton psychologists Janine Willis and Alexander Todorov reveal that all it takes is 1/10th second to form an impression of a stranger from their face, and that longer exposures

don't significantly alter those impressions.
So choose carefully the image you wish to
portray through what you wear and how you
act.

132. **Find Your Voice And Choose Your 3 Key Messages**
Have the courage to find your voice and
decide what will be your 3 key messages in
any meeting, or presentation you are giving.
Some people take up more time than others
and often speak in order to be clear about
what they think. Others are reticent to speak
and often think long and hard before they
decide to speak. Adapt your style.

133. **Power Posing**
Body language affects how others see us,
but it may also change how we see
ourselves. Social psychologist Amy Cuddy
gives a very good TED talk on how "power
posing"- standing in a posture of confidence,
even when we don't feel con dent, can
affect testosterone and cortisol levels in the
brain, and might even have an impact on our
chances for success. Choose your attitude
and your body posture.

134. **Mind Your Language for Deliberate Gravitas**
Ask a linguist and they will most likely tell
you that women often use more expressive
and emotional language, and use phrases
and words that soften opinion or gently
undermine a point so others feel more
comfortable. Words like "sorry", "I feel" or
even using self-deprecating language like
"I'm not an expert" or "Am I making sense?"
has the unintended affect of diminished
credibility. Practice using assertions and
persuasive language. Even if you feel the
language doesn't suit you, start step by step
to use it will help you build the confidence to
promote yourself authentically.

135. **Body Language**
There is much we can learn about reading
body language and being aware of the
messages we are unwittingly revealing
about ourselves. A Good start point is the
book What Every Body is Saying by Ex-FBI
agent Joe Navarro. It helps you to better
read the "tells", watch for people's baseline
behaviours and then spot anything that is
abnormal to indicate whether they're up,
down, or potentially lying. A good start point

is to study body language.

136. **Authentically You**
People can almost sense someone who is phony and inauthentic; it leads them to be highly suspicious and mistrusting of such people. Oscar Wilde quipped, "be yourself; everyone else is taken!" Further advice on authenticity is, "it is far better to be a 1st-class version of yourself, rather than a 2nd-class version of someone else."

137. **Networking**
Be selective in your hyper-busy world and don't just focus on the here and now and what's going on in the next few months. Think bigger: use networking to learn about future trends, broaden your knowledge, and enrich your experiences. Meet a diverse collection of people. Broaden and share your knowledge and constantly seek out best practice that you can apply to your own role from other sectors and walks of life.

138. **How Visible Are You?**
Google your name, see how many entries there are and how many, "hits" are

Leigh & Jonathan Bowman-Perks MBE

associated with your name and your role. Strengthen your web presence, social media, Twitter, business Facebook account and LinkedIn entries. Be clear on your messages and seek out speaking events and projects where you can contribute your unique talents.

139. **Begin By Changing Yourself First**
The only person's behaviour you can change is YOUR OWN. Do that first before you give advice, or criticise others. When you change your own behaviour permanently to be a more inspiring leader, then others will change around you for the better too.

140. **Humanity And Humility**
Inspiring leaders always keep their humanity and their humility and are more curious and interesting to others who buy them and all they stand for. This approach is far more successful than people who are self-absorbed, spending time brushing up their ego and overselling themselves by being too absorbed with self-promotion.

141. **Bin PowerPoint!**
Think carefully about your brand, reputation and image when considering presentations and talks. Unless you are an expert in using it, PowerPoint is neither powerful, nor has a point. Don't switch off your audience by thick decks. One page as a handout is best, however if you have to, then keep it to the smallest number of slides containing the fewest words possible.

142. **Give Others Credit**
"It is amazing what you can accomplish if you do not care who gets the credit." - President Harry S. Truman.

143. **TNT**
Never underestimate your impact on other people. You are always communicating whether you intend to or not. It is the TNT (Tiny Noticeable Things) that people always remember - about the actions you did, rather than what you said. It's always about the reality they observe, not your aspirational rhetoric. People learn YOU.

Leigh & Jonathan Bowman-Perks MBE

144. **Vulnerability**

Only the strong, inspiring leaders can be vulnerable. Be prepared to admit your mistakes and when you don't know, listen and be emotionally open in an appropriate way. It is far more authentic than the leader who bluffs and pretends to know when it's clear they don't.

145. **360 Feedback: What Do People Say About You When You Are Not In The Room?**

One of the greatest barriers to inspiring leadership and success through others is your lack of self-awareness and understanding of your impact on others. Get an independent person to conduct a 360 series of interviews, as well as using a 360-psychometric tool to get feedback on 3 key things: what is working well about you as an inspiring leader; what will make you even better and what people say about you when you're not in the room.

146. **Become Highly influential**

Daniel Priestley advises that if you wish to become a key person of influence there are 5 steps to become highly paid and highly regarded in your industry: (1) **Perfect Pitch** - succinctly explain who you are, what you do and where you add value (2) **Publish** - become an authority on your niche and subject (3) **Profile** - through speaking blogging, videos and becoming known (4) **Products** - your intellectual property IP that people value (5) **Partnerships** - collaborating with others to your mutual benefit

Leigh & Jonathan Bowman-Perks MBE

BQ Questions For You

1. What did your last 360 feedback tell you?
Get an independent person to gather 360
unattributable feedback on you.

2. What is your brand reputation and image?

3. How can you become a key person of
influence?
- Perfect Pitch - succinctly explain who you
  are, what you do and where you add
  value
- Publish - become an authority on your
  niche and subject
- Profile - through speaking, blogging,
  videos and becoming known
- Products - your intellectual property IP that
  people value
- Partnerships - collaborating with others to
  your mutual benefit

BQ Your Learning & Action

"In order to be irreplaceable one must always be different."

\- Coco Chanel

"DEEDS NOT WORDS"
LEAVE A SUSTAINABLE LEGACY
IN YOUR LIFETIME

LQ – Legacy

This is the legacy you leave behind after leaving the organisation. Your legacy is the impact you have made and left on your family, organisation, colleagues, community and society in the end. You may work with charities, develop others and enhance people's lives; things that make a sustainable difference and adds real value.

LQ
Role Archetype: Universal Steward
Stewardship
LEGACY
CHARACTER
VALUE-ADDING
COMMUNITY
Sustainability
Service
Customer
LONG-TERM

LQ – Top Tips

"In the UAE, we believe strongly that the empowerment of women is important to the future of our country. Without the complete participation of our nation's women, we will not reach our maximum potential".
Her Highness Shaikha Fatima Bint Mubarak

147. **Added Value?**
Once you have built sufficient trust and respect in your team and firm, then you have earned the right to ask the more courageous questions. One is "where do you add value?' Find out their specific skills and talents that could add real value elsewhere. Ask them where they think they could add true value and move them there. Tapping into your and other people's Passion = Profit.

148. **"Does It Add Value?"**
Use the litmus test of whether an activity adds value to your business and your customers. If it doesn't, don't do it. The Olympic rowers used to ask the question

Leigh & Jonathan Bowman-Perks MBE

of themselves, "Does it make the boat go faster?" And that was the key test on anything they spent their time on.

149. **Send The Elevator Back Down**
"If you're lucky enough to do well, then it's your responsibility to send the elevator back down" - Kevin Spacey, Actor. When life has generously rewarded you with good luck and success it's important to use that accumulated financial and experiential wealth to help others too. Positive change in the world doesn't require grand gestures, or extensive planning. Instead, people can promote social benefit in simple, yet effective, ways. Kevin Spacey encouraged others to do just that in the 2000 film 'Pay it Forward'. Rather than paying people back for their acts of kindness, 'pay it forward' to 2 other people, without expectation of anything in return, other than asking them to repeat the charitable process for 2 others.

150. **Adding To Society Adds To Your Success**
Inspiring leaders add back to society through involvement in charity work and giving of their skills, talent and effort. There is a direct

correlation between inspiring leaders and those people who make time to do things which benefit society.

151. **One Degree Of Difference**
Water boils at 100°C. It is extremely hot at 99°C, but it's not producing the steam that we need to turn the turbines. That extra 1° is what makes such a significant difference. The same is true about you and your performance - that extra 1° makes a huge difference. What will be your extra 1°?

152. **Your Legacy - The Final Countdown**
If you knew you had only 10 minutes to live how would you live now? If you had only 10 hours? If you had only 10 weeks? Or if you had only 10 months? Think about your legacy - you only have this life, so why not live the way you would if you knew you had only a short time left to leave a positive legacy.

153. **Survival, Success, Significance**
It is worth considering whether we are living a life of survival at the base level, a life of success at a higher level, or a life of

Leigh & Jonathan Bowman-Perks MBE

significance at the pinnacle. Which one are
you living?

154. **Memento Mori**
Memento Mori is the Latin phrase for the
philosophical reminder about the inevitability
of our own death. So we need to reflect on
what will be the legacy and what difference
will we make on our short time on this planet.

155. **Would You Choose To Follow Yourself?**
Consider the kind of inspiring leader you are
and spend time to: Prepare and Prevent to
avoid the need for Repair and Repent.

156. **The Mindset You Choose**
William Ward said, "We can throw stones,
complain about them, stumble on them,
climb over them, or build with them." Make
your choice to define the life you lead and
the difference you make.

157. **Be A "Silo Buster"**
When considering your legacy it's important
that you leave your team or organisation
in a better state than you found it. One of
the ways is to develop collaboration and

greater openness with other parts of your organisation and break down and bust up silos and small-minded thinking.

158. **Listen Without Needing To Be Right**
A small yet important legacy is the impact you leave on other people; especially when you truly listen to them. The problem is that as humans we often listen from the perspective of needing to be right. The result is we are not truly listening. So practice listening without needing to be right and you will ignite the thinking of the person you are with.

159. **Engage with The Future Pipeline of Talent**
Reach out to the younger generation and share your real life working experiences; you can take opportunities to inspire others, unlock their true potential and develop a pipeline of future professionals.

160. **Play The Bigger Game**
Betsy Hawkings shared a framed 'thank you' she had received from her friend, Beverly Eckart; Beverley was one of the leaders of the 9/11 widows group who sadly who later

died in a small plane crash outside buffalo in 2011. It said:

Do all that you can
However you can
In as many ways that you can
For as many people as you can
As long as you can

161. **The 2 Most Important Days in Your Life**
Mark Twain wisely said, "The 2 most Important days in your life are the day you were born and the day you found out why". What is your life purpose and why were you born?

LQ Questions For You

1. What do you want to be your legacy? How would you like people to remember you when you leave your organisation?

2. What would you like people to say about you in your obituary and when they attend your funeral?

3. What charity projects are you currently involved in and how do you give back to society?

Leigh & Jonathan Bowman-Perks MBE

LQ Your Learning & Action

"You can never leave footprints that last if you're walking on tiptoe."
- Leymah Gbowee

RUN PURPOSEFUL, SUCCINCT MEETINGS WITH
CLEAR DECISIONS AND ACTIONS.

Top Tips For Effective Meetings

As leaders we spend between 60-80% of our working day in meetings, often ineffectual ones! The deep cultural challenge is consistently one of the key areas that erodes leadership performance. To be an inspiring leader, it's time to intervene and call a halt to poorly managed and facilitated meetings. Here are just a few tips!

162. **Think**
     You are paid to think, not to be busy - shorten your meetings to create the thinking space that you need to be an effective leader.

163. **Purpose – Why?**
     Meetings can make people feel important. They create the illusion of activity; but the real work happens outside of the meeting. Be really clear on the PURPOSE of the meeting. If a meeting has no purpose, then push back and don't go.

Leigh & Jonathan Bowman-Perks MBE

164. **The 5 P's**
Planning and Preparation Prevents Poor Performance. Lack of planning and preparation (on your behalf as the chair) before a meeting should not become a crisis for the people who work for you. You spend time to save them time.

165. **Agenda Questions**
Turn your agenda items into agenda item questions starting with a "what" or "how" pre x - this will give people time in the lead up to the meeting to gather their thoughts.

166. **40-Minute Meetings**
Neuroscience research has shown that our brains tire quickly, so after no more than 40 minutes, take a 5-minute break and leg stretch and then start a new topic.

167. **Dump It And Be Present**
If you or other people have just rushed in from another meeting, without sufficient time to process what has been going on, then you need 2 minutes to dump or action those thoughts. This quiet moment allows them to jot down thoughts and actions from their last

meeting, which they can pick up when they finish your meeting. Then they will be fully present with what you need to achieve.

168. **WWW**
Always begin any meeting asking the question, "What is Working Well (WWW) in your work/personal life?" This technique is used in reviews and personal appraisals. You can also end any meeting asking, "What Worked Well in this meeting?"

169. **Dignity and Respect**
Show up on time for meetings and be completely present. Avoid the distraction of technology and focus on the task at hand and the people in the room.

170. **Are You The Oxygen Stealer or the Wallflower?**
Dial up or dial down your voice! Become aware of your impact on others. You have been invited for your leadership and so know you have a role to play. Give everyone have equal opportunities to think, contribute and speak.

Leigh & Jonathan Bowman-Perks MBE

171. **Commitment: Thumbs Up/ Thumbs Down**
Don't be deceived by the "knowing nod" when you propose a decision. Often such individuals then unravel your decision and disagree with it around the water cooler later on. Instead flush them out to show their commitment. Get a show of their opinions by actively putting their thumbs in the following positions: up to show support, sideways to show they need more information, or down to show that they are in opposition. You then need to ask those with sideways or down, 'What would it take to make it thumbs up?'

172. **When The Going Gets Tough**
...the tough get argumentative and the timid get passive aggressive! Watch your behaviours when topics become challenging. Take time out if necessary and reconvene with a fresh perspective. Do a round where everyone gets to share their freshest thinking for 30 seconds.

173. **Burning Issues**
At the end of every meeting give every person a quick 30 seconds to share any burning issues. These are topics that have

not yet been discussed, but are crucial to address at the next meeting.

Leigh & Jonathan Bowman-Perks MBE

"In my moments of doubt,
I've told myself firmly –
If not me, who?
If not now, when?"
   - Emma Watson

"Practice does (almost) make perfect: be as self-aware as you can be – of your strengths and weaknesses of course but also your behaviours. We all have good days and bad days; be mindful of what it is you do brilliantly on good days and focus on it to try and repeat explicitly, even when you may not be inclined to do it. Habits work; good habits are incredibly powerful and can become positive behaviours with repeated practice. Just as importantly, be aware of what triggers the less good or bad days. Each of us will be sensitive to different negative triggers. Recognising these is a key step to then working out how to counter-act or balance their effects. Being conscious of how we might react in a negative environment or circumstance; recognising the early signs (be they physical; mood or thinking patterns, for example) provides us with the opportunity to manage ourselves proactively. And if we still end up having a bad day, my key lesson is to learn from it. Taking responsibility for ones' actions is far more powerful than feeling guilty (or a failure) about them."

- **Elizabeth Corley CBE**, *Vice Chair, formerly CEO and managing director of Allianz Global, Member of the Microloan Foundation Women's Development Group and Crime Fiction Author*

About the authors

Leigh and Jonathan Bowman-Perks MBE

Trusted Leadership Advisors, Speakers, Mentor and Coaches for global corporations and their top teams.

Leigh and Jonathan have been described as, "a husband and wife power-couple who share a passion for bringing more inspiring leadership into the world". They are entrepreneurs who founded and run their own inspiring leadership businesses, based on many years' experience. Together they have created The Institute of Inspiring Leadership. They are very proud of their 4 adult children - in the Police, Teaching, Law and Psychology. While Leigh and Jonathan work and live in London and Lincolnshire, they love travelling to help leaders and charity initiatives globally.

Leigh published her first book "Inspiring Women Leaders (2014)" which shares her experience and captures a range of stories and wisdom from other inspiring women leaders and the challenges they are facing, have faced and have overcome.

Leigh is the Founder and CEO of our charity, the Inspiring Leadership Trust, where profits from this book are donated to.

Jonathan's vocation has been shaped by his Father's heroic leadership role modelling and his untimely death, as a British Royal Navy fast jet Pilot. His stories and experiences are captured in his book, "Inspiring Leadership; Leadership Lessons from My Life" (2010)

Leigh and Jonathan's life calling is to inspire leaders and teams to:

1. Find and live your "True North" (MQ)
2. Live your life "On Purpose" (PQ)
3. Leave a Legacy (LQ)

They are highly experienced coaches, executive team facilitators, motivational speakers, philanthropists and authors. They focus on current and aspiring CEOs, senior leaders and their teams in all sectors. They partner and collaborate with the best and brightest talent development specialists to support, challenge and inspire leaders around the world.

Leigh & Jonathan Bowman-Perks MBE

All profits from their books go to their charity the Inspiring Leadership Trust helping vulnerable women and children in London, Kenya, Nepal, South Africa and around the world.
Further details are on their websites at:

www.leighbowmanperks.com
and
www.jonathanperks.com

Leigh & Jonathan Bowman-Perks MBE

Key Contributor:
Nathan Newton-Willington,
Personal Trainer & Nutrition Coach

A special recognition of Nathan, our own person trainer, nutritionist and close friend (when he's not 'beasting' us!) who contributed to the HQ section of this book. Nathan's grasp of holistic health takes you beyond the surface of addressing physical health to the deeper stuff around mental and emotional well-being too! Email him at: nathan@transformationgenie.co.uk

> **"I was obese and used to be a car mechanic but I wasn't very good at that..."**
>
> -   Nathan Newton-Willington

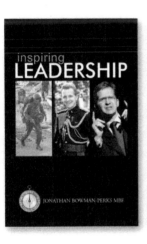

inspiring
LEADERSHIP

JONATHAN BOWMAN-PERKS MBE

INSPIRING
W♦MEN
LEADERS

LEIGH BOWMAN-PERKS

A HIGHLY PERSONAL INSIGHT INTO THE MINDS OF OVER
100 INSPIRING LEADERS FROM AROUND THE WORLD

Reference books for further reading

50 Years of Research in to EQ. Bar-On, Reuven

Drive: the surprising truth about what motivates us. Pink, Daniel, (2010)

Eat Move Sleep: How Small Choices Lead to Big Changes. Rath, Tom, (2013)

Inferno: the Divine comedy. Kirkpatrick, Robin, & Dante, (2006)

Key Person of Influence: the five-step method to become one of the most highly valued and highly paid people in your industry. Priestley Daniel, (2014)

Man's Search for Meaning: a classic tribute to hope from a survivor of the Holocaust. Frankl, Victor E, (2013)

Nonviolent Communication – A Language of Life. Rosenberg, Marshall, (2015)

Outliers: The Story of Success. Gladwell, Malcolm, (2008)

Quiet: the power of introverts in a world that can't stop talking. Cain, Susan, (2012)

Team of Teams: new rules of engagement for a complex world. McCrystal, Stanley, (2015)

The 7 Habits of Highly Effective People: powerful lessons in personal change. Covey, Stephen R, (2013)

"Penna PLC sponsored Research by Roffey Park in 2003 found that 70% of employees are looking for more 'meaning at work'. Those inspiring leaders who did created 20-30% more discretionary energy."

The Obstacle is the Way: The Ancient Art of Turning Adversity to Advantage. Holiday, Ryan (2015)

The Sign of Enough. Website http://signofenough.com/. Hart, Sara.

The Silo Effect; Why Every Organisation Needs to Disrupt itself in Order to Survive. Tett, Gillian, (2016)

The Speed of Trust: the one thing that changes everything. Covey, Stephen M.R, (2008)

The Tools. Stutz, Phil, (2013)

Time to Think: listening to ignite the human mind. Kline, Nancy, (1999)

What Every BODY is saying; an FBI Agent's Guide to Speed-Reading People. Navarro, Joe, (2008)

Willful Blindness: why we ignore the obvious at our peril. Heffernan, Margaret, (2012)

Some of our clients

IL-INSPIRING LEADERSHIP

IS YOUR LEADERSHIP STYLE INSPIRING, OR EXPIRING?

Lightning Source UK Ltd.
Milton Keynes UK
UKOW07f1426060317
295885UK00011BC/47/P